T0351456

Cargo Hold of Stars

COOLITUDE

THE FRENCH LIST

KHAL TORABULLY

Cargo Hold of Stars
COOLITUDE

TRANSLATED BY NANCY NAOMI CARLSON

LONDON NEW YORK CALCUTTA

www.bibliofrance.in

The work is published with the support of the
Publication Assistance Programmes of the Institut français

Seagull Books, 2021

Originally published as *Cale d'étoiles: Coolitude*, 1992
© Khal Torabully

First published in English translation by Seagull Books, 2021
English translation © Nancy Naomi Carlson, 2021

ISBN 978 0 8574 2 785 4

British Library Cataloguing-in-Publication Data
A catalogue record for this book is available from the British Library

Typeset by Seagull Books, Calcutta, India
Printed and bound by Versa Press, East Peoria, Illinois, USA

Contents

Translator's Foreword

Few books have had as great an impact on the course of my literary translation career as *The Parley Tree: Poets from French-Speaking Africa & the Arab World*, edited and translated by Patrick Williamson. This wonderful anthology introduced me to several francophone poets I subsequently translated, from an array of diverse countries including Djibouti, Morocco, Chad and Congo-Brazzaville. It was also here that I met Khal Torabully, from Mauritius, a critically acclaimed poet, essayist, film director and semiologist who has made it his life's work to give voice to the hundreds of thousands of indentured workers forced to endure horrendous conditions between the years 1849 and 1923. Indentured workers were brought from mainly China and India to the immigration depot in Port Louis where some either stayed in Mauritius as a cheap source of labour after slavery was abolished, or were sent overseas to the colonies to work the sugarcane fields. Many died on terrible sea voyages where they were packed in close quarters in the ship's cargo hold. Others died or endured harsh conditions in the colonies, where they were thrown in jail for the slightest offence, or were forced into longer periods of indenture. Torabully has coined the term 'coolitude' from the previously pejorative term 'coolie' in a way that resembles Aimé Césaire's coining the term 'negritude'. However, the poetry of coolitude is clearly dialogical in spirit and develops an inclusive vision of peoples, memories and histories of the colonial rim and distances itself from any essentialist inspiration. It is open to the humanities and differences that are articulated in a common oceanic song, beyond the *kala pani* ('black water') taboo.

Torabully argues that indentured workers, through their rich inter-cultural exchanges, developed a new identity and language greater than the sum of their parts—a strong and resilient identity worthy of dignity and pride.

The original French text of *Cargo Hold of Stars: Coolitude* (*Cale d'étoiles: Coolitude*) was awarded the Prix Jean Fanchette in 1993. In this ode to the forgotten voyage of a forgotten people, Torabully has developed a 'poetics of coolitude' or 'corallian poetics' that articulates cultural diversities and biodiversities through a variegated approach to indenture or coolie trade, necessitated by his conviction that ordinary language was not equipped to bring to life the myriad diverse voices of indenture. He has created a new French, peppered with Mauritian Creole, old Scandinavian, old French, mariners' language, Hindi, Bhojpuri, Urdu and neologisms. The playfulness of his language serves to underscore his deeply serious—even tragic—themes. Even the word 'cale' ('ship's cargo hold') in the French title of this book—*Cale d'étoiles*—is wordplay for the author's name, 'Khal', pronounced the same way. In order to bring the music of his poems into my translations, I employed a 'sound mapping' technique. First, I identified the salient patterns of assonance, alliteration and rhyme in the original, using a colour-coded system to help keep track within each poem, then tried to infuse this music into my translation without sacrificing the original meaning. Sometimes the most prominent patterns of sound involved an onslaught of wordplay, as is the case with 'Malabar'. The term 'Malabar' refers to Indians originally from the region of Malabar, India, as well as being a pejorative name for Hindus in Mauritius. The preponderance of linguistic acrobatics with the sound 'm' at first masks the serious subject matter until the reader realizes the writer's intent. Below are the first several lines of the original text, including the m-alliteration, as well as the more sophisticated wordplay of 'Malabar' and 'moi la barre' which sound very similar, except for the initial 'mal' and 'moi' ('labar' sounds the same as 'la barre' in French). Similarly, 'malais' and 'malaise' sound quite alike, and even look alike, but are not related in meaning and do not represent matching masculine and feminine forms of the same adjective.

> Malabar, moi la barre,
> moi motte de terre
> moi de sel moi de chair:
> mon âme lascar lasse
> quart malais tiers malaise

My English translation of these lines is as follows:

> *Malabar*, me the spar
> me mound of dirt
> me of salt, me of flesh:
> my worn-out lascar soul
> quarter Malay, third malaise

Another example of challenging word play is found in 'My equinox sails, my wails', where the original text includes the line 'ne me couvrez d'un unique perroquet', whose literal meaning is 'don't cover me with only a parrot sail'. The translation dilemma is that in French, 'perroquet' can mean either 'parrot', or a kind of sail, whereas in English, a parrot is a parrot. We don't have a 'parrot sail'. However, we do have a 'screecher sail', which seemed a way to approximate the combination of both meanings of the French word 'perroquet'.

To help the reader understand the meaning of unusual terms found in the poems, Torabully has included a glossary at the end of the book which consists mostly of Mauritian Creole, Bhojpuri and Hindi words. The translator's notes include other unusual words not found in the glossary, including neologisms as well as explanations of Torabully's very complex wordplay.

Of the more than 25 books written by Torabully, including the one commissioned by the Aapravasi Ghat Trust Fund, and put on permanent display in 2013 at this UNESCO-designated world heritage site, *Cargo Hold of Stars: Coolitude* represents his first book to introduce the concept of 'coolitude'. This publication represents the first time this book has appeared in English.

'Master mariners who sail the
Indian Ocean use something
that looks like a very thin and hollow iron fish.
When you throw it into
the water, it floats and, with its head
and tail, points to the two
directions of South
and North.'

Le Trésor des Marchands

Pages from a Ship's Missing Registry

Coolitude to lay the first stone of my memory among all memories, my language among all tongues, my share of the unknown that numerous bodies and numerous stories have lodged over time in my genes and my islands.

I ask myself if I'm part of a race of mixers, just like my forebears who blended spices and scents, silks and golds, pigments of skin and words.

Coolitude, my woozy-coolie, a song of rooting as much as a song of uprooting in an earth composed of other dusts, a much-needed encounter where Indians lend their ancient brass to the song of the world.

Here is my song of exile and joy to recount our journeys, our encounters and our endless métissage: before being reborn, I'm a man in the making.

Here is my love song to the sea and the journey, the odyssey my seafaring people have not yet transcribed.

In a language from *Île de France*, I therefore want to narrate my cargo hold of stars, go back to my ship in a harbour seen on a map. I already know that our song of waves, faithful as an amorous wound, can still sustain the backwash of our wanderings.

As if we were given invisible orders to take the journey to the very heart of human destiny, making it more about rootings than uprootings, community rather than rapine, friendly dockings at sea rather than scuttling and plundering.

In this new dawn, I steer my cargo hold of stars towards other horizons, hoping for such an encounter, so that my odyssey and my coolie journeys are not forgotten.

And I know that my crew will be among those erasing borders to broaden Humanity's Homeland.

Khal
Lyon, June 1989

For Hanna

I

THE BOOK OF MÉTISSAGE

'Now, the deep, dreadful, and lovely murmur
(. . .)
Teaches you the forgotten tongue
(With heavy and trembling syllables of dark honey)
Of Yasher's drowned books.'

Oscar Vladislas de Lubicz-Milosz

To a Coolie

If you had come from the sole contradiction
of an open wound in the sea
your exile would just be a rush of blood
to dizzy the islands' voyaging flesh.

But you come from a memory lost in advance
by a squall's sudden punch
by a reflex pelvic thrust of sense
a word of distress and silence
a memory forever recalled
in tomorrow's journey home.

Your death was suspended before your birth
for every woman you've never stopped loving.

And this woman is an island with saffron feet
whose blue womb is not a simple barrage
of bougainvillea or anthurium blooms.
SHE is the voice of your story, your life's void
memoired murmured for mixing of seas
voice consumed by the huge crater of reefs
whose last sigh is a beginning of poems.

You are of mixed descent to drown bloods
to recognize traits superposed
on the placenta's profound reflection.
You are an artist in need of an image
and your dance is forever
unknown by your roots.

You are a pure nomad of signs
key to your lips to open vertical words,

those that emerge from the very throats of the dead,
you are to be born in the friction of sheets
of our impossible islander syllables.

From these horizons of blood, of garbled words
your heated word capsizes clearness
in my memory's ocean depths.

My country will have no statue
of barefoot man-of-storm.
I've shattered my tongue against memory
when night cheated against death
in the game of boats and ports.
Here lies man-without-life.
Break the chains, smash the marble
and let all hands moor him to brass
to preside over the rise of tides:
my country will have no man-with-eyes-
dried-by-the-sea.

I don't believe I build borders
without us leaving the light—
dream
I am here all alone, a star
for your true inner gleam

and when the sea swell delivers to me
the blood songs from all humanity
you'll ask for my visa to enter the sun.

Carry my metaphor; I touched the sea
before the waves deceived me.
Carry my dream; I saw it all
without opening eyes of salt.
Carry my soul; I met death
but never ever died again.
Carry my silence; none of these words
belong to you
and I meld Indian words
with language from Saint-Malo.
At my Mozambican prow
a mélange of peppered dreams
is the aim of my human flesh.

Wound, may my mouth go dry
if ever I should die!

That's why I don't know the place
from where gloomy luggers set sail,
floating cables gripped by an ancient capstan—
what masts of dawn when blood throbs!

O may my mouth go dry
if ever I should die!

My equinox sails, my wails,
portholes drilled for dawn,
here I am, schooner-man with skin of wood!
Who will deck out my core, to the hatches,
who will flesh out my aloe words?
No, don't cover me with only a screecher sail—
to hear me, you need to reach me, o so fast
far from pitch, law is ditched. So many voices
squawk in my royal-sail blood: talk, bird!
The sunken coolie, the skinned man,
cut short, cut short, listen!
A fallen man become flesh!

I owe the cartographers
only my unknown journey's end
but not the stars or naked flesh,
for my vertebrae never saw the light.

I owe the sextants
only my flesh, de-oceanized of time
but not the waves or the dry wind,
for my mouth consumes the sea through its blue womb.

Lightning is a bit of burnt sky.
Better listen to me, standing my ground.
Dogs and cats
bury forgetting deep under blue paving stones.
Don't forget, island of mine,
that the first pigeon perched on my windowsill
was afraid to take wing in your eyes,
for fear of finding a cage inside.

A heart altered by alien land
knows that the sky doesn't stand still
and the azure is only fixed
to await the stars.

To imitate angels takes the slightest of shifts.

Language has coolied me
for conception, word of my spit:
pure cascade mixed cascade casket-bound.

Pure water pays no attention to bloodlines.
Cast clasped cloned:
guessing at what my next routes will be
is my true harvest of maritime dreams.

So sensitive were my welling words
that the Creole patois burned
my fibres: I lent my throat to the mute cry
of seamen torn apart by the whip.

My naked people, free of skin,
transplants of light!
And my lost legend
transfigures the island of stars.
Round bread slit bread
evokes my only home.
Beriberi
I know odysseys:
memory with no escape
is my path of sand.

Ahoy, I will be a referent of men
I will stand with the lot of them.
Ahoy, I will tend to the tingling of being
by tapping on my soul.
I'll take on all feelings of pogroms,
avatar of all chromosomes,
my light my burning *tawa*.

The moon sows white corals,
emptied masts relieved of shadows.
Ahoy
the waves are involuntary
in my eyes.
Ahoy.
My only homeland will be a human cry!
In each human wound, I will hear my race!
Ahoy, ahoy, ahoy!

If the sea
were cut off from the sands
I'd get it back.
If ocean foam
were faster than clouds,
I'd embrace it
on the sweet golden hooves
of the sun.
If the light were
ghazal
or mantra
I'd hoard it all.
The sea, Mahabharata!

No shore for water's drift in my dreams.
And the angel riding the backs of waves
wields a blue mirror
disfiguring faces of sailors on board.

On the *varangue* my tongue seeks a mango
and I'm harangued by a small topmast moon:
'Tell the tale of my curried crossing.'
O capstan pulley coolie
say light for truth.

On the *varangue*, mango under my tongue
I miss roll call (my heart reels)
how to steer the rudder
and give your flesh to all shores, all drifts, to your dreams.
O coolie capstan coolie.

Reef the sails, break the wind
of memories frayed by uprooted hearts—
I know this song, I know the odyssey.
O crating capstan coolie.

With my tottering soul
I came to know how the sky began
as far back as its root-the-light.
Fiery designs
will always lick my porcelain.

Each scar is a clear dawn:
even flesh, even the sea.

For all unbreakable bodies
my wounds will no longer return
to my blood, save for the ocean's waves.

I am not crystal
from the East India Trading Company.
I am human pollen
ready to tell of the cyclones again
in the screed of words.

My emblems are wombs and drums.
My beacon is in charge of the light of day.

And my eternity began
at the mooring lines of the very first sailor
on his glorious azure crossing:
not-to-be-uttered words, and all must be told.
I am human pollen
hitched to the helm of the sea.

I am, in truth, flesh fresh flesh
flesh flush with flesh?

For his feeler roots
like anonymous kings
Coolie was born beneath a banyan tree:
his tattoo is my only trace of forgetting—
my supreme delirium, my supreme attire.

White birds
are echoes of a sea of ash.
With your back more bowed, your hand more open
than the vault of the sky, o sailor,
sow your cries, red
from blood more solid than salt from the crossings!

And my sabre of blood
has cracked me to the core
and ocean vertebrae
have slashed my sails.

Define me please:
what's a Coolie?
One with a noose round his neck
denied the deck's cool lee side?
I am Lascar, *Malabar*,
Madras tamarind from bazaars,
Telugu with tell-tails for you.
Cruel Marathi mother or Chamar.
Whichever you like, I'm an Indian Black,
guinea pig, from Port Louis to Port-of-Spain
to replace mighty Zanzibar slaves.
For memory, my only *langouti*, a loincloth,
my language, purloined by the sea.
If you recognize me, please
call me proxy slave,
strawman or stand-in,
kapok from fields or ocean vertebrae.
But know that my sabre of blood
has uprooted me to the core.

I saw birth
long before the light of day—
like the coal man,
well before embers.
To distinguish each bird's
distinctive pure song,
I captured the light
in my closed eyes:
don't remove this flaw
that sizzles with rapture,
don't breathe new life into my roses
without a Persian tongue.
O don't leave me undone!

Capstan, call my ship by another name—
I only know the one of sweat.
This marine valley brands the dust
and changes the names engraved by the light!

Unreal mirror
that named me
unable to speak
like that strange scribe—
assassin of my shadows—
snatching the parchment page
from my body's extensive log.

The only womb I could bring along
if you even recall
was a stage curtain, white as a *motri*
(my receptacle of oracles, my coolie treasure).
The only womb I could caress
in the vast harbour of Port Louis,
(after a deluge of black graves),
a *motri* filled with dreams and rainy days.

The only womb you didn't give me when I left,
the only womb you gave me of exile,
o I couldn't bring it along and keep you alive.

My only myth
is the distance of native lands.
And my mother forbade me to pee
defying the horizon.
Why name each moment that aches
a sacrifice?

Dazed
a coolie
splashed an array
of colour on hatchways.
With a dab of his blood
without a bruise
the silent Scribe
plumbed his head into the azure.

Coolitude: because all humans have the right to a memory, all are entitled to know their first odyssey's port. Not that this port is a refuge, but because in this place, forever unnameable, they can raise those anchors that sometimes bind them to their truth.

Yes indeed, all humans have the right to know the flames that ignite their dreams and silences. Even to be their own history's moth.

By coolitude I mean that peculiar clashing of tongues which cracks the heart of hearts of millions of men for a history of crystal and spices, fabric and parcels of land.

Unsuspected music at the threshold of words from different horizons.

Within myself an encounter with those who invert the course of boats.

In a cargo hold of stars.

I could walk across red holothurians—
embers of ocean floors—
without scorching my skin.
A blow from the sea
did me wrong
abolished by chance
with a worse name.

Qu'y a t il dans un nom.
What's in a name.

I pray in inverted naves . . .
Kraken will grab me,
a narwhal will slice me up
but I'll gather the air
my *rôdeur de l'air*
tack upwind
yield to the tailwind
keep an eye on the abacus cleat
babouji broke the rope
lookout on port side . . . no
basbourdis guili guili oui
and all the sails will flap:
'You shouldn't cheat the sea.'

I cast anchor to keep a rendezvous.
Give me back these statues that stand
at the counter of froth:
the grinding of hinges is glair
on the moorings of memories.
Like wet nurses lacking ovaries
at sweet cardamom counters,
the merchant of Venice was weighing men
for the great chromosome mishmash.
O *sourti* trader, what kind of basmati rice
did you hand me for fragrant cry?

Hang on to my cord
drift in my ocean name
umbilical by measure
yourself a baptism of azure.

Hang on to an ocean sky,
my only lifeline after the rift:
o only boat
that adores me in my river-mouth core.

By monsoon admission
my basin is barley millstone.
In my pure bread of mélange
my throat's in a cargo hold of storms.

No I won't bare
my teeth.
No hope for me
to alter the dawn.
Between two chimeras
my name is a deeper blue
than the sea.
Inscribed on the ship's manifest
penniless man
hot-blooded
spicy ancestry.
Since then, at night,
I place seashells on window sills
to greet
boats without sails
on the front steps of our wounds.

Let's keep our memories mellow
for the ripe moon:
serrated name
fluted name
striated field
my bruised backbone
comb of a cock
wave on the sea
signal mountain
haughty handsaw!

O never again will I rush past death
in the casket of mollusc shells.

Only a gashed murmur of gangue
remains at this crossroads of salts.
I notice the sharp-edged tattoo
of a forked harpoon when my memory festers.
In the black of dawn, pure métisse,
my uprooted flesh will no longer give respite to exiles.
And my life's only protector is Death.

Forgetting is abrasion, sky is lesion,
and a coolie's stoop is distress
in the motionless transport of azure.

A *paan* is the sole ritual
of our only rage;
when we speak we chew our words
like crunchy betel nuts.
Each compression of our jaws
leaves a trace of deeper red flesh
in our only work:
sentences staining the sea.
No generous gesture
no unknown emotion
to stain our only language,
our lost blood, our true hymn!
Sandalwood scales
navel
porosity
lime means a burn
seditious lepidopteran
caliginous smoke
vaporous pagne cloth of a sail.
Chewing is our only ritual
rage our great muffled complaint,
its tattooing forever gone
from rot-resistant enigmas.

Here I am, o scribe of skins—
yes, a court stenographer, master orthographer—
graft my name onto nothingness,
my sombre body to epitaph.

Motri, I grasped you so tight with all my guts
that *catora* canoodled *carail*
and my soul seeded the last coral reef!

My muddy future is fully abulic:
soursop sops my flat-ribbed coast.
You are wrong, abolished by flesh,
your creeks crack when cutters approach:
tour abolie, tour à Bali
my backbone of kelp is the checkmate of masts.
Soursop sops my flat-ribbed coast.

When the sea vanished at last
like wizard's ink
I saw *Signaux*
casting its fires directly north.
My seaweed-filled dreams slid
toward the *Citadelle*, look-out of light,
and I set foot on land
like a bird fallen from a cage.
With my compass in my flesh
I touched my ship
yet never resented the waves.

Wordify me
soulify me
humanize me
manimize me.

Star, o my revolt of light.

My drifting dream restores your sign
when angels fall.

Star, o my lovely *grain lalin*,
give me your heart before morning.

Don't touch the djinns, don't ever again use rasps
to break the eyes of stones;
star, o my comely dawn,
your glance is a barrow of ash—
and the heavenly body burnt before the savage slash
of darkness
restores the gold of maps.

Silence travels a long way
to Médine Camp de Masque Pavé.
With every step my words turn humid:
here the sky doesn't hide a thing between my eyelids.
For what human escapes were beaches devised?

Malabar, me the spar
me mound of dirt
me of salt, me of flesh:
my worn-out lascar soul
quarter Malay, third malaise
will be fragments
broken cross-beams of sky
body broken
from setting sail.
To be a moutaille
I'll be undone, over there,
malady of mind
maligned Malayalam,
a lone me will be lost,
me so right, left to rot,
o memory.

Dreams of coolies, rust of pulleys
strewn with ropes for the sway of the boat
so many shadows to load dried spices
and wrack your backs with bullwhip kelp.

Speak, my *gouni*, tell my life story again.
'I was a black cat on a flour sack.
I was a padishah cat from the salt pans.'

My burlap bag
my blue talc
wove my sea wound.

Dhobi of slaves' dreams.
I was a dhobi of masters' memories.

Speak, my life.
'I was an orderly on the horizon,
Sirdar of kelp.
I was whole-man, anthurium,
harmony-man, harmonium.'
Repeat my name,
memory *moutaille* convolution:
'I was sheep-herder Ulysses.
I was plankton-race Ulysses.'
O tell me where I'm bound!

From coolie comes
my being kakhi, color of dust,
lachkar soldier of waves
I'm a diaphanous dragonfly
dunking my back into clear water,
lascar of salt water!

Aum acacia aurora
heave-ho my rickety boat.
Hallali halala
I crunch areca nuts.
Aum acacia aurora
I chew my only tobacco chaw.
Arrack, my betel leaf;
alalila alalila
my belly bloated with lime
to erode the legends of salt.

Aum acacia aurora
my spit thick as blood.
Balaclava—my catechu port—
I attract the red sea
to your burning bush:
I neglect to touch
the wavering golden sands
dawn's Swallow-man.

Swallow, take the rain
and give back sun:
malabar post-malaria,
malabar pre-*maloya*.

I found the sky
as I held my breath:
a bird cut across the night
with that thunderous sound
of a broken frail wave.

Gangrene paronychia
on my jelly legs!
For my pollen sweat
let only lead
be my just due.
At the rasp of brass,
since you all look half-crocked,
body and skin
ripe for the sacrifice,
hold hold the gangrene!
And so many bloods, so many salts . . .

Every human wound is my own story.
Beyond rice
winnow the trough
so my travels no longer blend with black salt.
Every human encounter is my true hope.
A mermaid
a chimera
a Mauritian.
An angel
a Human Being?

For J. G. Prosper

Masters' mighty prod
look away towards the window.
Womb missing from manifest.
Mauritius
the woman is a virgin.
Mauritius
my wife is a valve
Mauritius
my wife is a vulva,
Mauritius
my wife is invulnerable.
To free my hands
to handle the sugars,
heave-ho
my tracks strike back
heave-ho
my registered
rod.
My wife is a valve
my wife is a vulva
my wife is valid.
My daughter is vague
my daughter is vulnerary
my daughter is like a womb,
heave-ho
to free my hands
heave-ho
to handle the sugars
Mauritius
to suck on my hands.

My compliant backbone, able to corrugate
nights since my travels began,
could gauge golds and algae;
by now I know the angels of the north.

Hundreds of years will tile
the deep oblivion of foundered souls, our buried cries;
angels will tear out pages
from bodies, serrate names, torment fates.

Sawteeth sealed my doom:
lascar *malabar lansar*
cuddly *mazambique* madras.
And I offer my lower back as a holy-water stoup.

Don't be scared to catch
the *bolom sounga*'s tail
and tell the light you're sorry—
the sun will be my pride
burning all blood:
sun innocent bird.
Pure man, untainted by graves:
what fall from grace does the wind bring again
and this strange sensation
of this soft old word?
The sun will be my pride
to contract my womb—
pure caress, pure burden
depriving birth,
sweet ripe fruit, untainted by man.

I left for the mill
like a star ground
down by sweat—
and sweat duplicates dust
and your memory soundproofs crystals
and your shadow answers: wake up, sea!
I left at daybreak—
a genuine one-eyed sailor—
and the red bird
turned its head
towards the small mound of sand
I held in my other hand.

Earthy sustenance,
let my stomach take comfort from air.
Manna from watercress dreams
brings me the Kestrel
to sound the root and resound.

All the steamed *martin* and salted *sounouk*,
the broken rice drawn from my heart
disappeared in a single bite:
I built my dream
on rotten tiles
entrails of agar-agar,
my flesh is made of achar,
a human relish par excellence!

Anjali to pull down the star to my eyes,
the water babbles Anjali, tree-bound nymph at the riverside.
For the bronzed slain Angel, a strange place to die
in your sugars salted with sweat:
o your back riddled with holes from the strife.

A washerwoman repeats
my struggle among the pallial waves
she wants to rid the sea
from my all-too-dirty memory.

I fling a red mango
that makes the ocean impregnate the moon
(the little seashells
have not yet learnt to sing).

Wave to wave
balata: gum
Bengali wicker
Bislama for make-believe monster
bobeche ball padlock
sea in the sea
and I cut the *cadènes*
sea swallowing seas
and I wear the kaftan of tides
sea for sea
and my *calame* calms the winds
lightning rostrum
wave for wave
these shattered chariots of tidal bores
in front of the Central Market
and my camail and your fate
to moor the harbours
fishermen's nets
good lord
to rig
your head in the skin of the mast
wave within wave
to push the carambolas onto the sand
the *caye* of reefs
clepsydra of my song
colcothar on the season of salt,
connés: my two bodies welded with blood
my semen of stags
my absence of heirs
not a wave for a wave
not a wave on a wave

épouti on the small furrows
and my spinning top waltzes on spume
and my *glène* pushes land
further than land.

The gouramis will follow these exiles
until they can't yell: dance!
no backwash no arrack
indigo my load
julep my last tabla
minaret and naphthalene for trunks.

And wave without wave
rim-lock on the door of doors
parmélie without splitting the sword
unyielding courtyard
phalera on the upper deck
dipped in the sea without drowning
I will die at Phoenix
o wave for wave
and yet more wave than wave.

Trade wind on the fleur-de-lys of the wind
aluminium honeycomb
crawling on the sea to drown
wave without wave
aquilegia: archives of tides
aphthae of ships.

On the Island of Swans
I spill the sweat of the sea
as advance payment for hangmen.
Wave inside wave

mizzen mast: seats of the seas
aster: tomorrow's star
Indian almond tree amends the sand,
the sea speaks to slash the sea.

I want to go to the grand bazaar
to seek at last the saffron of shadows
o refrain from your refrain
the hoist of spices clears the remains
o refrain from your refrain
for your bodies heaped on the wind:
cries of cumin: cries my journey's route
cries of thyme: cries my future
cries of coriander corpses awaiting return.
And the bids of roots chased away
my terrified dreams all the way to hell.

For Lorraine

I am
the only runaway slave
who didn't flee the volcano's crush.
When coral raged
and the sky collapsed
the only runaway slave
who didn't escape.
I placed my flesh
in burning mountains.
I told the oceans
my cry is made of salt!

Because the sun
delivers shade to my door.

And the sea braided the wavy mane
of a nymph at nightfall.

And I sifted the sea
to gather all its salt.

II

THE BOOK OF THE JOURNEY

'My roots are in the Waters of the Ocean.
From there I have spread through all beings.'

'The Word', *Rig Veda*

Account of the Voyage

The sea gravitates towards my signal lamp
by the tall mast of shadows and stars
and I was a man at history's tribunal
when genesis had the jarring voice
of a Bengal tiger giving birth
and I was a man until torn apart
when recounting with steady words
the great journey erasing legends.

But the sea was reopened and the sea
was broken by a rudder's thrust
at the entry of a harbour without a country.

But the waves drew the mermaids
towards the portholes, towards the single fault
in my ship's vast mirror.

Before the fire was lit
for the dead before dawn
dark-skinned corpses were poured onto decks
before their chance to flee the ports
before they headed north to flee the pores.
But the sea in my soul is vast
and my ship's only davit is broken—
I was on the prowl on the prow, I was
above the sky and below flesh.

At dawn a spectre took offence
at the mysteries of mirrorless skin
and I said flesh was more than memory
syllable more than writing

and my absence itself a migration
through other bodies of coral flesh.

So sad was my other self who reeled
before the genesis of memories:
what happened to things washed ashore
and the rush of a moon on the waves?

What happened to my schoolboy slate
the silence of a night on the quays?

Without roundabout routes, I was arabesque-man
and your journeys and seas and dhows
and your compasses, beacons and maps
your stars counted before Love?

One night, the foetus in my trunk bled
before even decreeing death
but the sea presided over the candles
and the sea always comes back
to the only origins of day—
never looking the same.

And every sailor is a nomad
that death brings back to life.

Even so, his delighted eyes
stir the unreal mirror of seaweed laid bare.

Sleep in a hammock macerates ropes
that so many bodies braided for Loneliness.

Fearless, cut every azure thread—
touch the women tattooed on the mast—
and every porthole's a gap in the sky.

I write on the planks
of the ship
I hear water
racking its brains
as it slices through spume.
And first I gave away
my flask.
And then I placed my head
in the sky
to forget my empty hands.

Cast off with no shadow:
an army of strong *malabars*
sleeps in my dark cargo hold of stars.
Cut through the waves on the outskirts of Nicobar!
Charge at the great tidal bore, trim my sails!
In these souls like clods of earth,
carry my sacks with eyes of burning coal,
sow the sky in the furrow of seas!

Stow the horizon, mizzen spar,
in my ship of shadows, questions to spare!

When I coax from the throat
secrets divulged by monsoons
your basin is barley millstone
and my bread is pure mélange
of equator in cargo hold of storms.

For Denise and Christian

I rein in the boundless night
by the torch of your veins;
at every artery known
your mermaid heart
hails me as nomad of waves.
O voyage, my only word of love,
your blood is carnivorous:
your bright vessel
caulks my flesh.
And let the weary night graze
my dark skin
and steer my journeys past
the shadowy holds.

Brothers, many a time
my eyes have trembled
tilling the tides.
Brothers, many a time
my hands have failed
counting lightning strikes
that lashed ribbed, coral coasts.
Once, a sudden gale
made me flee through the faults
of my frozen vaults.
Brothers, many a time
the crossing became my only retrieval
of entrails.

Our cargo hold is a territory
that's lost our birds:

let the muffled sound of bedsheets
make the light call out between our dreams.
Only the sail is unnerved
by a woman's cry.

And your mouth is a ripe syllable
that only the imprint from words of love
allows me to kiss below your lips
at the very heart of a broken sky.
And you say OM.
Why follow a siren
who lacks your tender hands?
And I say hOMbre,
may my skin in response to your carnal call
reel off words softer than your breasts.
OM OM OM
and to think of a woman
while at sea
and from so much absence be lulled.

No grammar can express
the blood of men.
I chew my syllables of flesh
which splash the sea.
Even the thunder has turned
beguiling and sealed
like the mouth of the sky.

And I far-fling the spice
annoyed by the lookout-less night
and fervour the mouth
which kisses me until midnight words,
but I keep the sun to rub out
the stars on musty maps,

for it's blood that my temple pounds.

Step lively seamen
cast some ballast on top of my skin
avoid a void o vacant hold
each cargoed body has grounds
to hang its eyes from the bowsprit.
Poor buggers—
compost of luggers—
with no tiny three-cornered sail to resist the wind!
Avoid a void o vacant hold
we are journeying lèse-men.
At our feet the sun rules out shipwreck.
At the slightest shade from the topgallant sail,
avoid a void o vacant hold.
For my only diversion,
my flesh is the cordage of continents.

Om
but the sea swoons
with delight in holy purity
but sand breaks the stone
that covers my face

who will perform my ablution
before the dirty waves?

I aim to blame blood.
Why didn't you free me from sulfur?
On Île de la Passe
my element traces
erases
my journey by sea.
For
at last I'll be able to dream
of a trial in the past tense.
O *paille en queue*
take heaving seas
and make coolies.

I aim
to remake blood.
O *paille en queue*
take back the depths
give back the flesh.

In the future limbo
of your flesh,
my dreams might recount
the lustre, a comet's tail of seaweed.
Through the burning blood
of eclipses,
a sea fairy will be my coralline *pari*
when my very first one dances.
Steer my spar
through the ocean, so slow and so long.
For
in the limpid nave of a breeze,
dawn's light veil,
I lit my lamp of clay
to mingle your mouth with the salty wind.

For Bernard Prédignac

The rigging repeats
its slicing motion through the ocean's thigh.
What audacious crew
braved the belly of the wind
crossways through the storm?
Commotion of eyes, sole complaint of the stars,
and every lookout is a landscape thief.
At the tiny gateways to mainlands,
with our wanderings for only weight,
our blending of bloods
adds our pure exiles to the absent ones.
Cargo hold of stars contrived
scar, mouth of embers—
as penance, our parted lips
engrave these phrases on open seas.

I've always heard
islands through hatchways:
hanging from a silver yardarm
to weave the shrouds,
why do I have a masthead ache?

Captain, distant god,
put away your azure whip!
And next, before break of day,
I'll hang my drum's mirages
on the large rungs of waves.
And next, before love,
in my trade-wind cargo holds
I'll blend for you
fresh water and salt water.
And next, before break of day,
I'll be a man dispersed
by a great gust of wind.

And so close to trade-wind cargo holds,
before albatross and spider crab,
I'll be another fit of rage.

And the moon
dog-tired
sank at low tide
in a sopping crackle and pop.
The sea said these words
that drove our soul
out of its body?

O parhelion—sundog—my *pari*
parching wind in Delhi
skeleton keel, coral-reef chock
fish-scale cable, port of call flesh,
horizon deeper than sea.
My sundog of pure gold
my compartment of three aepyornis plumes—
when northern squalls rushed
to my compass of thirty-two winds,
the gale from the change of course
returned to reclaim my laughter:
steamer trunk, steering wheel
to caulk my name
through the crammed cargo hold.
O parhelion, my parry.

To G. Loumeau

You have the same clear blood
that opens the shutters of shrouded dreams.
Can we abolish everything, even the sky,
when we forget the dead?

Everything comes to a halt in the heart of the waves:
soldiers rinse their quivers
in my shifting concavities.
Long before land is proclaimed
their shields deflect
the silk of rays onto the heads of kings.

Everything comes to a halt on wrecks of ships
when coal-bearers bathe
in the great blaze of dawn.

And shadows whisper as clouds parade past:
everything comes to a halt so we can be told
of the night of a drum of flesh.
And let me see the seashell stairway,
let mermaids drag me in their wake!

Count the wind
by the whacks of the keel.
Cut the waves
by the stabs of the reefs.
And the heaving waves that come to a halt
are heavy oxcarts.
What pyramid made of basalt
is taller
than these sea-spray typhoons?

All my tools for working the earth
all my iron birds
fall apart in the harvest of waves.
Heed the wind
as it furrows the sea?

The sea
shrivelled,
spun
spume on my upper deck,
poop and prow.
For mooring,
kedge anchor,
grapa pine trees of iron,
malabar with dandy cane
to lash
my matte-skinned race.

As my flesh is caulked
I want to change dreams:
in dry dock at each port of call
my blood flows to the Strait of Malacca and sinks.
As my skin is traced
within memory's enclave,
cry burning lava, my blazing banner.
O body, you have my life:
corossol vocable, obole vocable.
Waves be damned!
My blood is incense
anchored in ink.

I have faith in the rhythm of waves,
in canticles of salt, *qawal* of ocean froth;
the sea will claim that her dancing alone
will make seashells sprout feet.
The land will claim that incense and praise
will generate legs on a seahorse.
I have faith in the tabla of swells,
in the storms' strong *ravannes*.
For the cosmic cadence
of midnight poems,
the ocean turns sega, flow's motion is crazed
when shuddering blue ignites:
the wave was a woman of fingers and soul.

Ahoy from the blue boat:
how do you lull dusk to sleep
without shutting the eyes of the untouchable orb?
Without passing through to the other side of the sky
and making a ball of sparks?
Ahoy from the gangway of wind
where the light absorbs me to such a degree
that thinking makes me live on in my soul.

I know from now on that my wound
will be found where dawn cripples dreams.
The sun in my chest
to blind me to eyelids
I barely know:
o close your eyes
when you look at me down in the hold.

For André Gérin

As in a dream begun again,
the ship is preceded by unreal tears,
its cargo of corpses delivery-bound
through a bleeding horizon's soft slit.

Deep down in the hold, what eyes
can discharge their despair
without springing a leak on all sides?

Star, *cythère cythère panaris.*
O night skies, so clear
that when I lay me down in the sea
I'm released to my ultimate country.

Your two hearts forever apart
make us remember this strange endless time:
not once in my uprooted life
did I suffer from so much forgetting.

But in the gleam of glabrous chins,
I stopped all the chitchat;
we started to hunt
for Mira, Aldebaran, so we'd never forget.

I no longer have a piquant shadow
far from all those names coated in ash:
who danced before Queen Apsara
nacreous hips, spark of massala?

Star, *s'y taire s'y taire panaris!*

The lookout chases sea stars
like nearby birds;
these strangers have no mast.
But their tainted solar tint
will recognize salt, will narrate the waves,
lonely great faces dismissed
to emptied salt flats.

Do you know the tale
of the lonesome man
in the East India Trading Company?
His skin was lit with sparks
salt-pond pores
on a rainy night.
To the pearls of spume
his voice became an almanac
for seasons of exile.
Often this man
returned to the seas
on the *dalo* of his wound.
Sometimes along streets
of lost waves
he blows out stars
on his china divans.
Often long blue rattan
brands his flesh with algae
from the horizon's only shipwreck.
To ignite the dawn
of crystal cries
this loner
sells iron stoves
in the paved courtyard of lagoons.

For Geneviève Turille

This cinnamon scent of life
moves between homeland and rainbow,
your presence is pure sunlight
borne by a picture of bees.

From even your pure dream falls
the soul of another, the soul of others
like light, the heart of day—
may your own past emerge
from a broken spice, a forgotten word,
massala, my salty one!
At the prow, I vanquished the yellow sea and left
to hear your secret revealed by the birds.

Lodestone attracting dreams
compass rose sliced into thirty-two rhumb lines
portolan chart begun from the stars,
and in our heads
astrolabe disks, edges marked in degrees
dissect the skies.

Alidade guide since the Coromandel Coast
revealed the regal star's highness
unworthy above our brown skins.
And I hid my graph
of the sun's declinations—
recovered cross-staff
eternity's goldenrod—
and my hollow fish
took me back in their golden fins.

In Memory of Poivre, from Lyon

Burning Albuquerque in Goa
at the cape of storms
without hope,
stealing spice from the Maluku Islands
and ripping up Marco Polo's book
my gaff sail muslin of wind,

the only mission I didn't fulfil!

The vessel led our star into the tidal bore.
Crumbs of leaden light dispersed
into the flesh of jellyfish and rays.
And you went on and on,
saying I shouldn't invent
shadows cast by crustaceans' feet.

Each rudder will be my sabre of dawn—
a hard turn of the tiller will wed my dead dove.
With every port I see,
my memory gains a new corpse.
The vessel sometimes pitched, sometimes tacked
towards the void
and to stay alive
a man cried out 'Steersman,
from the horizon, seal our fateful stars.'
And for good reason, plied with ether
my name will be inscribed
in the ship's log of the living-dead.
And since leaving means to put down roots
in another land
I'll be born after a time:
I'll thread my way through the waves.

And for the sake
of uprooting our scapular clays
the boat of brown stars
was reflected in waves:
since then, in the face of the sky
emptied by sudden typhoons,
bamboozled men resembled droplets of spume.

Without a spurious memory,
the sole true blood, like salt
flowed around
every white seashell
wrenched from the belly of languages.

Speak so as not to forget—
isn't this the true gift of tongues?

For the Castaways of the Ker Anna

For the first time, we were naked.
Who taught us to fall from the tree?
What power had we wasted?
To which blood founding our fables?

How many frantic birds will flock
to the bulwark of our awkward lips?
How many dreams will be razed
when we are subdued by the storm?

Bury me quick
before I die.
All the birds of lightning
have wept a long while
too slow the stone
too furrowed the heath
in the bee find your cleft.

Without knowing how,
I woke up
in a cargo hold of stars.
Too harsh the ocean
too sure the flesh
in the exile find your suture.

My soul has sailor's mange,
and my fingers sport ploughman's calluses.
Eyes kept closed
so that nothing is seen before dreaming:
every fluid fate knows
the weight of what it reflects!
Gong and sistrum, handbell and Santhal drum
before prenatal doubt:
the sea impregnates my memory with song.

The sea wilts for the drowned.
And mermaids perform their ablutions
when camphor wafts by.
O praise be to phosphorus
whose legend interred
the stars in my native land.

Our foremasts don't measure
the gaps between stars.
Sometimes our cargo holds seem to grasp
the intimate immensity
bridging our skies and our eyes.

My cadastre of flesh
dissects me right to the bone:
coal lustre, eyes lined in khol.
And a virgin's red nail
will arrange the sky
with a pure and transparent sunset.
Will you find surveyors
among your steamer trunks of salt
to measure the depths of tidal bores?

O lookout, observe the boreal man
in a gouging of flesh;
two arpents of flesh
slash my ocean dreams.
I confide in the salt,
distressed by its wounds:
I inquired after the sky.
Now my crossing
has reached Le Morne.
The moon at its peak
rode a riddle—
my purulent flow.
Billot heavy with blood,
I call for the corpus of coral—
and the sea fell into a shell. Salaam.
So long Sooty Man, namaste!

O call my voice
but don't answer me back any more.
When we hoe the waves
I pay no mind to the weight of the sails.
At the bow or the keel
my eyes excavate furrows
ahead of invisible islands.
Jellyfish and onyx people,
I want to hear you say:
my proud absent woman
my proud present woman
yes, keep your ending
for someone else.

For Raza

I'll smash all the astrolabes made of gold
so children can be born
far from chains of lead.
My plumb flesh hooks exile—
my banished blood
won't allow me to ease my fables.
Qui ferre? Qui ferre?
Lost without sun,
my three eyes shut,
I speak without grief
of my water wound.

So many days go by
and I'm dying of fright.
Deciphering love
helps pass the time.
Qui ferre? Qui ferre?

Ah, if I could escape from your hands
to deny Columbus my ovaries,
yes, escape from your loins
to deny Nelson my lower back.
Set me free from my only backboned batallion!

Que faire? What to do?
Toss myself overboard,
true to the exile I choose?

Ship's hold is my flesh of spice.
Ship's hold is my flesh of space;
from the point of view of the virgin word
my skin is to blame.

Ship's hold is my cry of the human race.
Ship's hold is my memory, full-faced;
a taste of sand on the peephole,
every cry takes my scalp.

Like spume, each body
wakes up on a wave.
One straw, two straws
four score sepoys
and for entrails
a coulis of blue men
paw through
stone-clotted fields.
We are molasses, we are bagasse
my African brother descended from slaves
our skin is the trace
like yours, of the same dark race.
One straw, two straws
four score sepoys
for full-face deduction
devalued by French tarot
man tied to the tides
by the spar made of coconut wood
a flaw falters
a man without seeds
destitute die-rolling race
hanged from pandanus trees,
in the name of the stunning sea

And the cabin boy dreamt of the last bypassed reef
precipitous crack of waves at my cliffs!
There the coral night lightens the load of the sky,
and its wound blames me for its embers!

The hatch: my thick veil for thinned marrow,

the steersman thought, to slice the split horizon.

My copper face was overhauled from silt
at the first stripping of blood and flesh.

Our only wanderings wiped off the portolan charts,
said the cabin boy to every drooping face.
And this country's name was my fate:
Pointe aux Piments, Cap Malheureux, Triolet!

Therefore, I go to the land of my birth
where nothing remains,
and my eternity lived,
I yearn for a large shaded garden.

Here we will name you rainbow—
like honey, you came
in the midst of rebirth for pollens and wings.

Friend, I'm staying here—
a long night
knows no end.

Insular, insula, Insulindia,
insult, insulin,
I couldn't hear, I will not align the words
(you killed me so much to hurt me).
Quay-bound careening cargo hold.
Carriage of stars,
so many dreams to purge of stones.
I didn't touch your flame
to avoid caresses:
insufflated scalped insufficient
I've wished so long to be a man of every race.
And I heard myself fall
into the haze.

To move the ivory sentry
I touched the clear sky mirror.
A root
cosmic egg
with two leprous sores
rises from a nocturnal cove:
without matrix of confession
as far as the other sun
mytonguewithoutanation
surprisedmeinitsdazzlingblindness.
Forwithoutspeakingofthevanishedabyss
only the sentence is a cicatrix-matrix.

III

THE BOOK OF DEPARTURE

'And the sweetness of vedic times
Is still alive in me.'

R. E. Hart

And they slaughter the seahorse
at the height of their despair.
And they fondle the octopus
to purge it of tales.
And thanks to our fruitful struggles
the sea multiplied space.

Then they sorted me female or male
human by species
to perpetuate
my prayers for rain
in the powdery sea—
seven from every line of descent.

But the sea delights
in divine cleanliness.
But sand breaks the stone
of our overwrought faces.

With our cinnabar seeds
to rise in the open seas,
the ocean is finally ripe
for lasting harvests.

I pick up the mortar
I pick up the pestle
I crush the season's pods.
O my azure drums.
O my grains of salt.

My saffron wife
hitched to the nautilus,
my hennaed fay

hitched to the frothy waves
my myrrh-perfumed lover
snatched from the wings of fish.

My book of farewell
is purer than death . . .

In the thousand and one nights
of a first voyage by sea
I rubbed my lamp of waves
on your passing isle.

The nomad likes to watch
the orchard, the traveller
likes to get back to his fruits in the night.

Yet already I remember each golden scale
stuck to your hands—
woman is a seascape
her water sac is a first voyage
woman is a vessel
her blue flow is a tide of flesh.
Every-woman is a map
(with only the route left to plan).

Obsessed with placental loss
man has always wanted to leave
for the furthest reach of the sea.
And woman knows that the ship
is the only great cradle
the wind can tend.

Some birds
watch us dream
others search
the sky
and prefer wider windows.

I will load the conchs
onto the backs of swans.
And almighty light
I will sort your signs
as if black lentils, without
defacing the manuscript signed
by the waves.

Our departures don't measure the gaps
between absences.
Sometimes our windows seem to grasp
the intimate immensity
bridging the skies and God.

My cargo of mother-of-pearl decks out the sand
to seep in deeper than light
and erupt as dust.
Without banning my banners
and breaking wave after wave
I'll ascend again for as long as God.

Song of the Envoys

For Sir S. Ramgoolam

Come, you from the Grand Peninsula
To tiny *Île de France*.
Come dance the unbounded dusk
To make your face and senses pure.
Here is the Island of Rupee, the Island of Cash.

Just pick up a stone and be rich.
Here all masters are friends.
Come for all the gold of *Dwipa Aropi*.

When I heard this great call
A vessel led me away to heaven.

The envoys told me
Come to *Île de France*
And take *Savane* and *Coin de Mire*.

And the transoms of waves
Opened and closed the azure
On the horizon's pure sail.

To cover the distance across the Indian Ocean,
Our ship will glide for ten days,
Closer to you than the beating of blood.
The ocean? No worries: sweet as a lover
When our ship reaches the last reefs.

And I'll know after two drowning moons:
Time was the burn of hours.
And I'll anchor in Durban, *Dina Morgabine*,

Singapore, Mombasa, Nairobi, Toamasina,
Trinidad, Fiji, the West Indies,
in the dust of the waves.

And scatter myself across continents' winds.
Along currents of colonies.

For J. M. Fournier

I've seen the sea, the pond,
bees, compasses,
triangles, zithers—
designs of starfish
I measured
with your golden rule—
and in the green water
I saw trees
give shade to the stars.

Before forging through
firm sea, firm mother-of-pearl—
scar from now on—
I seize the dawn
without wavering
wearing my turban of waves.

If only my mother
had told me about the sea
even on a monsoon evening
when, on the roof, the kelp
was sighing under the wind's scythe.
But the poor woman felt
the earth down to her blood,
and to make the night fall
in our eyes, she would rise
to reach fig, lemon,
mint, her sweet potion.
If only the earth
could tell me the words of the sea!
Yet one night she spoke
of a great coral monster birthed
by dreadful waves, of a depth
more abyssal than our murky hallway.
She told me you lose your temper at waves
she told me you get impaled on coral
she told me you run yourself aground on algae.
And yet on the roof, if she's to be believed,
a boat capsizes with each gust of wind.
And yet as she tells it, when she's seen,
seamen remember her strange screams.

O my mother, from what dread
were my ancestors pulling away: fear
of too-near horizons, flying fish
prouder than our two Indian peacocks?
Or fear of setting forth for this Somewhere Else
where our blood forgets
its solid colour, abandoning homeland wombs?

You'd heard the true tale,
legend of men lost in the orchard of gales,
swept overboard like five black sous.

You were birthed in the tide's flood
I thought, the water was here long before us
to commandeer Wandering.

And the monsoon confused you in its ropes
when the last village madman spoke
of a book more strange than a shipwreck.

You from Goa, Pondicherry, Chandernagore, Konkan, Delhi, Surat, London, Shanghai, Lorient, Saint-Malo, mix of people from all the ships who brought me towards another me, my cargo hold of stars is my nautical chart, my space, my vision of the ocean all of us crossed, though we didn't see the stars from the same point of view. From gangway or deck, no voice but mine told me my part of the journey.

In saying coolie, I'm also speaking of every voyager barred from a ship's registry, all who've ever embarked for horizons of dreams, whatever the ship they boarded or had to board. For when besting the sea to be born on another shore, sailors on one-way trips like to plunge back into their stories, legends and dreams. The years before memories were formed.

On my gangway at the edge of the stars
you knew the swell would sweep me away
further from your fate than mine
and myself.

As pleased the sky, you'd repeat moray eels.
The sea is a spooky boogeyman.
As pleased the salt, you'd whisper sirens.
The sea will overflow fountains.

In your eyes now more soaked than sea spray,
you wanted a land, you cried hell
with no portolan chart for each child,
for my children.

And throw death to the wind.
Any cascade of gold in the dead of night
is not the only tattoo of your eyes
the schooner that leaks all the salt.

For Henri Queffélec

I'll touch your hand
where harvests die
so that one day the sand
may at last open the eye of stones.
I summon the light when the star succumbs.
And you'll say brother sailor,
may a cast-iron mummy
brandish a broader hand
to hold back death.
And at last to leave the sun, I'll say
we'll inscribe the flesh of love as if we were the same!

The night was clear
like a single ovarian scream.
This unreal mirror, this serrated field—
unreal, this dance of channels,
yet my true horizon.

The night was clear
like the last exile of craters.
A page ripped in two by arms of the sea
threw me from my ship of stars.
Clear ovaries,
why serrate the sea?

I don't think
playing hopscotch
at full half-light
will unleash a lightning bolt
in your eyes;
I don't know if the stone
your voice pushes
sunward
in the rainbow's
soft sobs
will relieve you of your womb.

To play hopscotch
your body must leap
into the light
to wear out death,
and to shout at long last,
your mouth will be flesh
more alive than your soul.

For I. Banian

In our stories of sandmen
black coral is a lingering shadow.
Turning our eyes towards the wall,
salt is a jewel box, sea froth its pearl.

In my former country of light
stars guided streams,
and a woman diverted the sea
so that each distant word was for me a tearing.

For Camil

Sonorous seaweed has forgotten the sea
pic pac through our fingers
to puncture the wind.

Each child, to forget your breasts,
has loved a woman.
The images dyed the waves
pic pac through their dreams.

Will forgetfulness matter when we
can no longer remember?
At times, hands forget
fingers meant to caress you.
Pic pac my child
to shatter my journey's remains.

O woman, the crossing is darkness
softness of a warm star
scorched in a nearby sky.

The hand doesn't plan
for every small pore of passage:
that's how water and storm
lie down in delight and lighten the sky.

Evening, hard rider
with brass spurs
to draw blood from my furrows of gold:
absence is the only distance
felt by the heart.

For Alain Wesbuch

Whisper:
voiced dream of a vacant womb.

Murmur:
girl unaware of birth.

Cry:
woman breached by a departing child.

Space won't give us the chance
to depart.

Freedom won't hold us back
from renouncing death.

Memory won't hold us back
from recalling without grief

that every new start
is for us an exile
and exile is the only trace we leave.

For Jeanne and Edmond Masson

I know the echo, I in-grave the sea,
I chase after dazzle, I spellcast algae.
And I don't know, I no longer know
if the horizon absents flesh.

I absurd the burden, I squander silence,
I cover skins, I square white stars.

I lose the spume, I lose the loam,
and all the moorings of scents
are only loosed for the skins of our love.

With no ransom to spread out the clouds
the first words tumbled
like pebbles on the dust
of the storm.
And my dove, lost in a lightning flash
anchored my dreams and ether keels.
Anjali said, the vessel is scuttle-prone
from our hasty departures
before the handkerchief raised
by a nail-eater
a sword-swallower
someone who walks on fire.

And my syllable is a still bridge
where north takes back south again
as far as the cardinal point of the bird.

Anjali, the only imagined ghost:
and at the mandolin's sound
may your chest rise in a star's fine reflection
to soothe the mothers of my crew.

And yet on the seas
you drew me away from women—
to keep my dreams from burning
you opened my eyes:
on your East India Trading Company's
translucent china,
I tattooed the bloom
in turquoise hues.

With this gesture, my fate,
last bird, will leave you
for fins of shooting stars—
and will spread in the swell
seven domes of salt
and your last siren call.

A stone took on my defence
as its only emblem:
o leaning against the sea
with a bundle of waves!

And if I chose a vessel with strange accents of the sea, it's because I want to be at home everywhere else, even in words most removed from my borrowed soul. The doors of the world have been knocked down for me by a current-of-blood and a drift-of-flesh navigation.

Coolie, because my lost memory chooses its roots in my truths.

But I only seize this tongue insofar as it adopts me, to no longer be blocked from the word.

And, at the threshold of French, I vary the way, I knock in a different way on vowels and consonants. First and foremost I love words, even more than my wounds.

And I speak my French tongue to point out my home port on the map of my discoveries. Marriage between my oceans and continents at last.

The sea eats its sons
and I will crunch stones
and not cleave the maim
nor believe the snail.
And the sea no longer runs dry
by man-made decree.
And the junction of waves
bathes the crosses
in nebulous lights.

In my great saga of blood
the sea is cruentation of seaweed.

For Gandhi

The horizon was a pink more delicate
than the first seashells' exquisite skin.
And the sharpest of stars, by chance,
began to invent sea urchins on the sand.

Shadows whisper as clouds parade past:
everything comes to a halt to narrate the heart of a trial,
the night of a flesh drum.
Let me see the seashell stairway,
glimpse the ultimate motive for why we set sail.

Night will shower the hidden flowers
with shade's long embrace:
what gathering place for exploded stars
among endangered spaces?
So our hearts may be exposed
a bit further than our senses,
I'll go myself to sow your blood
as far as the Gorgons' magnificent eyes.

Pacts retract, concede to creeks
to the strict act of coral reefs
and crack the keel once more
when crying out: which port of call for the anchor?

At this moment, my heart expands:
my legend of gold will not enter the Indian Ocean
beyond the embryo of ether.

For the moment, my body overextends:
in the fine sand, who sells talismans of salt?

My legends will not go past
the embryo of moths.

At the prow of wordless waves
I remember your shadow
passing over these statues
to read the real death.
My flesh is colder,
your dream in miniature, more real.
Wait, through the breeze.
Wait!
Before I depart
through the azure door.

My skin sings more than I do. That's why I was born in a country whose name is inscribed in the sea. My skin speaks more quickly than my voice. It is my true weight.

That's why my cries are the backwash of men captured by silk, exiled by nutmeg and rooted by sugar. By islands and colonies.

My skin is caulking for my flesh, and all the memories carried by pitching masts.

My song is therefore coolie; my coolitude is my only share of a memory tossed by the waves.

In the wakes of boats sowing men at the end of the world, I want to speak of my burden as a man and my flesh of ink. For my words were watching as open-hulled ships sailed by.

I refuse
to leave for a dream that takes too long—
the schooner falters
and I've neither sky nor vertigo.

But I speak to the void.

We're from an ancient home
where goldsmiths hoarded their loot
in large ebony trunks.
Their eyes, narrow caskets for jewels,
parried dubious suns.
A cutlass at their back,
bearers of waves with each backwash,
they refused
to depart on your boats of spume—
and departing and nevertheless
our only fate
departing is all at once
the balance owed by our roots.

Before, to tell about leaves,
I'd watch the wind.

Before, to close the sky,
I'd draw the curtains.

And to absent women,
I'd picture their birth.

O never before the wound
had I suffered so much from my senses!

To the nacre darker than my flesh
so that the star finds the full-fledged
sea, give me a single name flushed
with light on my marrow's flesh.

I don't believe seizing the amphora
spreads the seeds of clay lamps:
in each great coral reef, shadows lose their way.
You are there
all at once—
like a bright fruit,
plant by birth.
When the lamp sails away
in the deepest gloom of things,
I'll look for a backdrop darker
than the absence of waves.
You left all at once
and phosphorus purer than azure
showered my skin with razor-sharp shavings:
who ran you through with a ghastly echo?

Since the grey sky will come crashing down
I return with my body, horizon-bound.
With my navel as keel of dawn
I'll know by heart how to steer my flesh.
Hush up cloud, hush up storm,
the first voice will weep in the sea.
For beings who've disappeared, hush up:
the flight of beings augurs BIRTH.

For L. S. Senghor

Coolitude: worker bees of the colonies; you were merchandise, and we, merchandising, or vice versa.

Coolitude: because my shores teem with new traces of memory. And if African gestures came to our hands as we cut the cane, the cracking and dancing of fingers remained ours, used to the tabla, often attuned to the ravanne's *great cry of hearts adrift.*

Coolitude: because I am Creole by my rigging, Indian by my mast, European by my spar, Mauritian by my quest and French by my exile. I will always be elsewhere only within myself because I can only imagine my native land. My native lands?

In our tongues, we're at the fertile frontier of codes, to hear a word among the exchanges of masters and slaves. Is this why my true mother tongue is poetry? Why my only native land is the Earth?

That's why I am ready to quell all border quarrels so all may see our star and share our common heritage: flesh and blood.

Coolitude: not just for the memory, the past of our first crossing of Earth. But also for those human values amassed by the island from encounters with sons and daughters of Africa, India, China and the Occident.

My only dreamt homeland: the great brotherhood of humanity, of reconciliation.

For this part of ourselves that we must compose in the light of day, with an eye to human destiny waiting to be fulfilled. Once again I propose we be porters of futures, worker bees of worlds, sowers of languages, builders of bridges connecting continents poised for a healthy sharing. Know yourself so you can build better together. For memory regained is a great plan for the future.

What other truth can there be that carries the weight of a word handed down from the ship's lookout post?

A Few Words from the Land of My Birth

Achar: spicy Indian pickle made from green vegetables and fruit.

Agar-agar: a kind of edible seaweed used as a vegetarian substitute for gelatin in many Indian desserts.

Alalila: Creole word, meaning 'here it is.'

Anjali: sugar-factory worker killed during a worker uprising in the 1930's.

Apsara: dancers and courtesans born from the churning of the sea.

Aster: Creole word meaning 'now'; pronounced the same way as the Latin word 'aster', meaning 'star.'

Babouji: a Hindu of a superior caste; sometimes used in the sense of 'master'.

Bagasse: the pulp left after juice is extracted from sugarcane.

Balaclava: Mauritian city of Arab origin.

Billot: block of wood supporting the keel of a ship; a cutting board in Mauritius.

Bobeche: cup or ring that holds a candle in place in a candlestick or candelabrum.

Bolom Sounga: Mauritian boogeyman.

Cadène: chain (in a nautical sense).

Calame: reed writing implement used in ancient times (from the Latin).

Camail: Provençal word, referring to piece of chainmail attached to the headpiece and protecting the neck and shoulders.

Cap Malheureux: a village in the northern part of Mauritius.

Carail: cooking utensil used in frying; diasporic version of Indian *kadhai*.

Catora: utensil used for eating; diasporic version of Indian *katori*.

Caye: Creole word, meaning bed of coral, as well as filth.

Citadelle: military fort overlooking Port Louis, the capital of Mauritius.

Coin de Mire: town in northern Mauritius; also known as Gunner's Quoin.

Conné: someone born with two organs fused together.

Corossol: tropical fruit with a strong flavour.

Dalo: gutter; originally a hole in the side of a ship for the runoff of water.

Dina Morgabine: first name given to Réunion Island, from the Arabic.

Dwipa arobi: one of the first names given to Mauritius, from the Sanskrit 'Silver Island'.

Épouti: garbage.

Glène: shape of the cordage when it is coiled.

Gouni: gunny sack made from jute and used to carry sugar.

Gourami: fish of the Indian Ocean.

Grain lalin: flaxseed, used to make a refreshing drink; burned, it is used to chase away the evil eye.

Langouti: a loincloth worn by some Indians; also spelt *langoti*.

Lascar: sailor from India or Southeast Asia, derived from the Persian 'lachkar' (soldier); pejorative term for Muslim Indians in Mauritius.

Maloya: a kind of music danced and sung in Réunion.

Marathi: Indian originally from the region of Maharastra.

Martin: a kind of bird or a Mauritian vegetable.

Médine Camp de Masque Pavé: a group of villages in Mauritius.

Morne: coastal village in the southern part of Mauritius.

Motri: Indian word that refers to a large bundle, usually of possessions and bedding.

Moutaille: Indian fried sweet, shaped in coils and steeped in syrup.

Paan: betel leaves stuffed with slaked lime; when chewed, it makes lips and teeth turn red, and has stimulant and psychoactive effects.

Pandanus: tropical tree, vacoa (screw pine).

Pari, péri: a creature of paradise.

Parmélie: a small round shield.

Pointe aux piments: a Mauritian village on the coast.

Qawal: song in a style of Muslim devotional music associated particularly with Sufis.

Qui ferre, Ki fer: Creole for 'why.'

Rhumb: measurement of the angle between two of the 32 points of the compass.

Rôdeur de l'air: Creole word, meaning onlooker or gawker.

Savane: a village in southern Mauritius.

Signaux: refers to Signal Mountain, overlooking Port Louis.

Sirdar: Persian word ('sir' means 'head' and 'dar' means 'who possesses'). Used as a title for British officers in Egypt, it can also refer to a foreman leading a crew of workers on a plantation.

Sounouk: a variety of salted fish.

Sourti: someone hailing from the Indian port city of Surat.

Tawa: circular frying pan used to make flatbreads in India.

Triolet: largest village in Mauritius.

Translator's Notes

PAGE 4

The pejorative term 'coolie', once used to refer to indentured workers, mainly from India and China, was revitalized by Khal Torabully and extended to encompass the richness of transcultural exchanges (geographical and cultural) throughout the world.

The term *métissage* refers to the blending of distinct elements, including a biological or cultural sense.

Mauritius, under French rule between 1715 and 1810, was known as *Île de France*—island of France.

PAGE 15

Varangue is a French word (as well as a Hindi word) that means 'veranda'. It also refers to the floor plate of a boat situated perpendicularly over the keel.

PAGE 23

Basbourdis is an older term that was used to refer to lookouts on a ship, on port side.

Guili guili oui is said in the context of tickling a baby.

PAGE 27

The pronunciation of 'tour abolie' (abolished tower) is a near homophony for 'Torabully', as is 'tour à Bali' (tower in Bali).

Kakhi is the Creole term for khaki.

Mazambique is a pejorative term for Black people in Mauritius.

Lansar is a Creole word from Mauritius that means a 'saw'.

Swan Island is the name given to Mauritius by Domingo Fernandez, a Portuguese navigator.

Lèse-men is my invented English word to approximate the French neologism 'lèse-hommes'. Both terms echo the expression 'lèse-majesté', the insulting of a monarch or other ruler.

Île de la Passe refers to a small Mauritian island captured by the British from the French in 1810.

The *paille en queue,* a beautiful bird from the Indian Ocean, is featured in a Mauritian nursery rhyme: 'Quand il pleuvait, paille en queue prends la pluie et donne soleil'—'When it rains, *paille en queue* takes the rain and makes sun stay.'

Fall is a time of stubble burning and sundogs which the ancient Greeks believed were portents of storms.

PAGE 54

Grapa is a troubadour word from old French that refers to a hook. In Brazil, it refers to an unfermented drink made of sugar and water.

PAGE 55

A *ravanne* is a large tambourine-like drum made of goat skin, whose sound can be heard in Mauritian Sega music.

PAGE 57

Cythère cythère panaris is French for the Creole expression *siter siter panari*, a children's game. *S'y taire s'y taire panaris* is wordplay pronounced in the same way, meaning 'say nothing, whitlow'.

PAGE 59

The hollow fish shape of needles was used in compasses of the Arabic-Islamic world, dating back to the thirteenth century.

PAGE 60

Pierre Poivre (1719–86) was a French botanist who introduced spice plants to Mauritius by smuggling them out of the Dutch Spice Islands.

Afonso de Albuquerque (1453–1515), Duke of Goa, was a general who secured the Portuguese monopoly on spices from the East. The Cape of Good Hope was originally known as the Cape of Storms.

PAGE 62

The *Ker Anna* was a French ship that sunk in 1804 off the coast of the island of Réunion, a French colony in the Indian Ocean to the southwest of Mauritius.

Sir Seewoosagur Ramgoolam (1899–1985) was a Mauritian statesman and philanthropist after whom Mauritius' main international airport is named.

The peacock is the national bird of India.

Henri Queffélec, greatly admired by Torabully, stated that 'all men are sons of sailors'. He died before he could write the preface for *Cale d'étoiles: Coolitude.*

This poem is dedicated to Torabully's son, Camil.

Pic pac comes from the French version of the Disney song 'Heigh-Ho', from *Snow White and the Seven Dwarfs. Pic* refers to a miner's pick axe. It is also the sound Mauritian children refer to when describing the sound of algae air sacs exploding between their fingers.

Translator's Acknowledgments

My unbounded gratitude goes to Catherine Maigret Kellogg for her expertise and support in translating some of the more difficult texts. I am fortunate to be one of the beneficiaries of her recently completed graduate translation studies at the Sorbonne. I am also indebted to Khal Torabully for his patience, insights, and friendship as I worked my way through the translation. In addition, thanks to Danny Lawless for allowing republication of an earlier version of the translator's foreword that appeared in the February 2020 issue of *Plume*. Special thanks go to the small, but mighty editorial team at Seagull Books, led by Naveen Kishore, for their dedication in bringing this book into existence while working from their homes during the coronavirus pandemic. Finally, I am very grateful to the editors of the following literary journals in which versions of these translations first appeared:

Agni: 'And every sailor is a nomad'

American Literary Review: 'Captain, distant god', 'I know from now on that my wound', 'I left for the mill'

Another Chicago Magazine: 'I aim to blame blood', 'Om', 'Our foremasts don't measure', 'O woman'

Asymptote: 'A heart altered by alien land', 'And the moon', 'And the sea braided the wavy mane', 'And your mouth is a ripe syllable', 'I found the sky', 'I owe the cartographers'

AzonaL: 'A washerwoman recounts', 'Capstan, call my ship by another name', 'Here I am, o scribe of skins', 'O my mother', 'May my mouth go dry'

The Brooklyn Rail: 'And if I chose a vessel with strange accents of the sea', 'The horizon was a pink more delicate', 'If the sea', 'In the thousand and one nights', 'So sensitive were my welling words', 'With no ransom to spread out the clouds'

Circumference: 'Bury me quick', 'Each rudder will be my saber of dawn'

The Common: 'Only a gashed murmur of gangue', 'Speak, my *gouni*', 'To move the ivory sentry'

Copper Nickel: 'Anjali to pull down the star to my eyes', 'My naked people', 'With my tottering soul'

Delos: 'Every human wound is my own story', 'In the future limbo', 'O parhelion', 'Space won't give us a chance', 'Whisper'

Diagram: 'And the cabin boy', 'As my flesh is caulked', 'Cast off with no shadow', 'Don't be scared to catch', 'I rein in the boundless night', 'Star, o my revolt of light'

Gargoyle: 'And they slaughter the seahorse', 'Gangrene paronychia', 'If only my mother', 'Sonorous seaweed has forgotten the sea'

Guernica: 'My cadastre of flesh'

The Henniker Review: 'Hang on to my cord', 'I cast anchor to keep a rendezvous', 'The only womb I could bring along'

The Literary Review: 'For the first time'

Los Angeles Review: 'Dazed', 'I will load the conchs', 'Masters' mighty prod','My muddy future'

Metamorphoses: 'Count the wind', 'I've always heard', Lightning is a bit of burnt sky', 'Pacts retract', 'Pages from a Ship's Missing Registry'

Mid-American Review: 'A *pan* is the sole ritual', 'Earthy sustenance', 'I don't believe seizing the amphora', 'The lookout chases sea stars', 'My compliant backbone', 'My skin sings more than I do', 'This cinnamon scent of life'

New Poetry in Translation: 'In our stories of sandmen', 'The vessel led our star into the tidal bore'

Pleiades: 'No shore for water's drift in my dreams', 'Unreal mirror', 'Wordify me', 'You from Goa'

Plume: 'I could walk across red holothurians', 'I'll smash all the astrolabes', 'Lodestone', 'Malabar', 'O lookout', 'The rigging repeats', 'Wave to wave'

Poet Lore: 'No I won't bare', 'The sea'

Poetry International Online: 'And throw death to the wind', 'Dreams of coolies', 'Insular, insula, Insulindia', 'My soul has sailor's mange'

Prairie Schooner: 'To a Coolie', 'For his feeler roots', 'My country will have no statue', 'Some birds', 'White birds'

Seedings: 'Ahoy from the blue boat', 'Before forging through', 'Before, to tell about leaves', 'Burning Albuquerque in Goa', 'I've seen the sea', 'Our cargo hold is a territory', 'The sea wilts for the drowned', 'To the nacre darker than my flesh', 'When the sea vanished at last'

The Southern Review: 'Coolitude: worker bees of the colonies', 'Language has coolied me', 'You'd heard the true tale'

Transference Literary Journal: 'I have faith in the rhythm of waves', 'I know the echo', 'I refuse', 'My cargo of mother-of-pearl decks out the sand', 'Night will shower the hidden flowers', 'No grammar can express'

Transom: 'As in a dream begun again', 'Everything comes to a halt in the heart of the waves', 'Step lively seamen'

Two Lines Online: 'Account of the Voyage', 'Ahoy, I will be a referent of man', 'I write on the planks'

Waxwing: 'At the prow of wordless waves', 'I am', 'I want to go to the grand bazaar', 'My equinox sails, my wails', 'Star, *cythère cythère panaris*'

West Branch: 'And my saber of blood', 'Coolitude: because all humans have the right', 'Do you know the tale'

World Literature Today: 'Carry my metaphor', 'Like spume, each body', 'The sea eats its sons'